NUMBERS IN DREAMS

DORIS SNYDER

BALBOA.
PRESS

A DIVISION OF HAY HOUSE

Cover work done by Quillan Snyder

Balboa Press books may be ordered through booksellers or by contacting:

Balboa Press
A Division of Hay House
1663 Liberty Drive
Bloomington, IN 47403
www.balboapress.com
1 (877) 407-4847

Because of the dynamic nature of the Internet, any web addresses or links contained in this book may have changed since publication and may no longer be valid. The views expressed in this work are solely those of the author and do not necessarily reflect the views of the publisher, and the publisher hereby disclaims any responsibility for them.

The author of this book does not dispense medical advice or prescribe the use of any technique as a form of treatment for physical, emotional, or medical problems without the advice of a physician, either directly or indirectly. The intent of the author is only to offer information of a general nature to help you in your quest for emotional and spiritual well-being. In the event you use any of the information in this book for yourself, which is your constitutional right, the author and the publisher assume no responsibility for your actions.

Any people depicted in stock imagery provided by Thinkstock are models,
and such images are being used for illustrative purposes only.
Certain stock imagery © Thinkstock.

Print information available on the last page.

ISBN: 978-1-5043-6720-2 (sc)
ISBN: 978-1-5043-6721-9 (e)

Library of Congress Control Number: 2016916015

Balboa Press rev. date: 01/18/2017

DEDICATION

To my loving parents, Hedy and Arthur

CONTENTS

FOREWORD

When asked to write the forward for this book on numbers, I initially thought it would be a simple matter of writing my opinion on a subject I am fairly well versed in. As a Jungian psychotherapist and spiritual director, who works with the metaphoric meaning of the dream as it applies to one's daily life; I have been pleasantly challenged by the depth of information offered here.

I believe numbers offer us valuable information related to our psycho/spiritual lives. Numbers are resources to consider in our exploration of our dreams as well as synchronistic events in waking life. How often have you noticed a repetitive occurrence of a number, such as 1:11 on the clock and then on a license plate on a car in front of you?

In "Numbers in Dreams", Doris has combined a wide range of information offering the reader a resource to apply to both "waking and sleeping dream work". She has researched her subject matter to a depth that offers all readers, be they novices or professionals, insights that are worthy of deep consideration. Included with the information, this publication offers the reader the opportunity to record and reflect on numbers as they have appeared in their dreams, thus offering a workbook as well as a resource.

I find the information extremely relevant personally and professionally and an important tool for working with numbers as they appear in life. This is a book I will not hesitate to refer others to use to deepen their associations and experiences with numbers.

Diana McKendree
Jungian Spiritual Director and Dream worker, Senior
Faculty of the Haden Institute

"The very numbers you use in counting are more than you take them for. They are at the same time mythological entities (for the Pythagoreans they were even divine) but you are certainly unaware of this when you use numbers for a practical purpose."

G.C. Jung[1]

INTRODUCTION

A Beginning

My life changed immeasurably when I first learned about dream work. All it took was a glance at a poster in the window of a coffee shop in Davidson, North Carolina that was advertising for a dream class. Standing in front of the poster I could feel my pulse quicken. It was a recognition, at the core of my being, that this was something that I wanted to do and had always wanted to do. I quickly pulled out my cell phone to register for the class. Little did I know how much that simple call would change me and my life.

Signing up for the class led me on a journey of self discovery unlike any I had experienced before. It was thrilling, rewarding and scary. The class connected me with people who have deeply enriched my life and continue to be part of my "tribe" of folks who get this journey deep within us. Dream work has also given me purpose and direction when I needed it most.

None of this was known to me when I showed up for the first class. The ten class participants were a disparate group of men and women. We shared our basic bios and what had brought us to this dream class. There was a poetess, a retired chemical engineer, a youth minister at the church where we were meeting, a divorced musician raising three teenage boys, a bubbly and creative business woman, an executive lawyer with an affinity for Native American culture, a housewife with college-age kids, and me – a certified spiritual director with a life-long interest in dreams. The facilitator, John, was a minister with a degree in Depth Psychology. He headed up the Counseling Center of this large, progressive church, which was sponsoring our class. John's calm, low-key, southern gentleman-ness made us feel less nervous about sharing the most innermost parts of ourselves - our dreams. Nonetheless, we shifted in our seats when he brought up the meaning of sex in dreams. To our surprise we would learn that sex is a metaphor for the merging of contrasting aspects of yourself. Sex often represents psychological completion. For some of us, it was a relief to know sex in our dreams did not mean we were being, in some way, unfaithful to our spouses or partners.

It wasn't long before our small group became a sacred gathering where we would share our innermost selves through our dreams. Each of us took a turn facilitating the gathering. I loved what the dream work was doing inside me: tapping into creative areas I did not know I had. It is no surprise that I still stay in contact with some of these dear dreamers.

Jungian Connection

John had us read books by and about Carl Gustav (C.G.) Jung and other practitioners deeply entrenched in dreams. The material was all new, fascinating and profound. I wanted to dive in deeper and so I signed up for the Dream Leadership Program at The Haden Institute. Offering programs in both Spiritual Direction and Dream Leadership, Haden is a beautiful sanctuary that melds together Jungian psychology, spirituality and mystical traditions. The Dream Leadership program is a two-year program designed for people who desire to go deeper with their own dreams and learn how to lead dream groups. The course reading material is similar to many degreed programs in Jungian psychology. I came away with a strong Jungian perspective on dreams, a firm grounding in dream history and symbolism, and experience in leading the dream group process.

Dream Work is Soul Work

Dream work is not a casual undertaking. I learned quickly how the dream world contains a rich and imaginative landscape providing beautiful images, amazing figures, and delightful events. It is also a complex, confusing, and sometimes vulnerable and scary world. Yet when we carefully sort through all its layers of hidden meaning and deep emotions, the dream world offers us a direct path to understanding of our truer selves and soul healing. As my dream mentor, Diana McKendree, often says, "Dream work is soul work". There is such truth to her wise words.

Midway through The Haden program, I noticed that many of my dreams included numbers, particularly the numbers 3, 5 and 7. I began to wonder why they were in my dreams. What purpose did they serve? A quick search on the internet pointed me to information on the meaning of numbers in numerology. This was helpful but left me wondering how to apply that information to my dreams. Looking back, I now see that this was a pivotal moment for me. Again I felt that inner nudge to go forward and dig deeper. I decided to explore the topic of numbers in dreams in my final paper at The Haden Institute.

"Numbers are the sources of form and energy in the world"

Theon of Smyrna, 2nd century AD, Platonist mathematician

"Archetypes are not mere concepts but are entities, exactly like whole numbers, which are not merely aids to counting but possess irrational qualities that do not result from the concept of counting, as for instance the prime numbers and their behavior. Hence the mathematician Kronecher could say: Man created mathematics, but God created whole numbers."

C.G. Jung, Letters[2]

POWER OF NUMBERS

Having numbers appear in my dreams came as a surprise to me because I don't have a great relationship with numbers and mathematics. I transpose numbers all the time. I was terrible in math in high school. My eyes would glaze over when the lectures started. It was a foreign language that I could not understand. For some people, the opposite is true. Numbers speak to them; there is even a fondness for what numbers can do. There are some people who truly experience numbers in a way unique from most of us.

For example, some people on the autism spectrum have exceptional visual and academic skills. Autistic savants often have unusual and heightened sensitivity to numbers. There are also people with synesthesia, a neurological condition in which two or more senses entwine. For them, numbers are often experienced as a sound, taste, smell, shape or even color.

Everyday Use of Numbers

It is undeniable that numbers play an important part in our everyday lives. We use and memorize an array of numbers - Social Security numbers, birth-dates, bank accounts, cellphone numbers, passwords, etc. Beyond the obvious uses, however, numbers also have important, deeper and sacred meaning. But we have lost connection to these spiritual qualities they possess. This was not the case for most of history. Numbers inspired wonder eons ago.

Lost Wisdom

In ancient times, numbers were held in high esteem and were integrated into philosophy, art, religion, and architecture. Numbers were viewed as inherent and visible throughout nature and the universe. Because they facilitated the growth and transformation of consciousness, numbers were considered sacred.

Pythagoras, a mathematician, philosopher, and creator of Numerology, believed that numbers provided a map of our own inner psychology and sacred spiritual essence.[3] Each number had a life of its own and unique role in the universe. Moreover, in both numbers and nature he saw the same divine imprint. "Strip away all the sensory features of color, texture, tone, taste and smell from an object and only number remains as its size, weight and quantity. Take away the features associated with the number and all is gone. Ordinary numbers and shapes represent eternal verities in a form made comprehensible to us."[4]

This wisdom was shrouded in mysticism and secrecy. It was taught orally only from teacher to pupil partially to avoid conflict with any prevailing intolerant religious authority. Overtime, this wisdom remained obscure and was discussed only as part of the divinatory arts, such as astrology and tarot cards.

For most people today, numbers have a narrower focus. In our culture, numbers have power from their place as rational and objective tools. We have expressions like "the proof is in the numbers" or "numbers don't lie". Numbers and rankings are everywhere. On the internet, you can find rankings for almost anything: colleges, best cities to live in, fantasy football, the top 10 healthiest foods to eat, etc. We make important decisions like which car to choose or where we will retire based on rankings. We are obsessed with quantifying everything. However, our limited focus with numbers may result in our overlooking more ambiguous things like wisdom and expertise.

Fortunately, some of us intuitively understand what the ancients knew: that numbers have a deeper meaning in our lives. We have not lost touch with this wisdom completely but we have put it away like an old book on a dusty library shelf. Recently I had to close my lock box at the local bank because the branch was moving. I had to complete the paperwork for a new box. But this time I was surprised when the branch manager asked me if I had any number(s) that I wanted for my new box or were there any numbers to avoid. Here was someone clearly in tune with the power and meaning of numbers.

Some of us have lucky numbers and use them to play the lottery. There are numbers that people and even societies avoid, which explains why many hotels and office buildings do not have a 13th floor and many airlines omit the 13th row in seating. *Triskaidekaphobia,* or the fear of the number 13 is a widely pervasive fear. Friday the 13th is considered by many to be a very unlucky day. Evidence of this phobia can be found in some pre-Christian traditions. The Mesopotamian Code of Hammurabi, a Babylonian code of law that dates back to 1760 BC, omits the number 13.[5]

Awareness Today

Some of us have an awareness of numbers in our daily lives. I have a friend who suddenly became aware of the number 5 and then started noticing its appearance in multiple places. Why? What is the significance of this number? My sister will tell you that in the course of a week she very often looks at the clock and the time almost always is 3:33. Why this number?

A friend, who has Asperger's, dreams frequently of large strings of numbers in the billions. It invariably reduces to the simple number 6. Why 6 and why now?

My son has a thing about the number 11. He believes it holds strong meaning in his life. He is very tuned to seeing the number and understands its significance. In numerology, there are master numbers that have profoundly powerful meanings. The master numbers are 11, 22, and 33. The number 11 is a master number that resonates with spiritual enlightenment and creativity. It is also the most intuitive of all numbers. My son has two of them in his birth number. When he found out what the number 11 meant, it was a confirmation of what he knew intuitively. He recently graduated from art school and hopes to bring his art to a wider audience.

Sensitivity to Numbers

The level of sensitivity to numbers varies with each person. This has enormous implications for consumer behavior. Corporations understand this and spend millions of dollars researching brand names and numbers. They know that some numbers work and others do not. This is part of semiotics or the study of the powerful meanings hidden away in cultural signs and symbols. Greg Rowland, one of the founders of this discipline and The Semiotic Alliance, has helped the biggest brands find fame and fortune for their companies with semiotics. Rowland was interviewed by the author and math blogger, Alex Bellos, and shared some of his experiences with several major corporations including KFC.

> "The number 11 is an essential element of KFC's corporate mythology: its signature fried chicken is seasoned with Colonel Sander's secret original recipe of 11 herbs and spices…. According to Rowland, 'This is a key mystical use of the number 11 in commercial culture'. [6] What does the number 11 mean? Rowland says that 'Eleven is opening the door to the infinite and transformation; one beyond the ordinary.' [7]

Doris Snyder

Statistically people have an affinity for certain numbers. Scientists have shown that people are more attracted to odd numbers than even numbers. In a study by Yale University[8], students were asked to give the first number between 0 and 9 that came to mind. The number most chosen was 7. The reason for this remains unclear. Is it due to the fact that the number 7 has a long history across cultures and that our own biological rhythms are tied to seven days of the week? Regardless, we have a sensitivity to that number which serves companies like the 7 Eleven franchise well.

These cultural associations are part of our internal landscape. They reveal themselves in our affection or connection to a number that we cannot explain. It is not surprising that they are part of our dreams.

Is there a number that appears to you regularly in waking life and/or in your dreams? Is so, start jotting it down. Use the space below to record anything that comes to mind.

Keep track of this. As you go through this book you will hopefully gain some insights into what the number means. It will enhance your understanding of your dreams and your connection to that number.

The number 7 appears in my dreams with regularity. Why? What is the significance of this number? My research for my final paper at The Haden Institute gave me the answer to this question and more. As I will share with you shortly, it showed how much numbers inform our waking lives and our dreams.

CHAPTER 2

NUMBERS ARE ARCHETYPES

When I was in the Dream Leadership program, I was living next to a wonderful college library with a helpful and professional staff. I was surprised that the library had virtually nothing on the meaning of numbers in dreams.

Jung's Theory

That night I widened my search for information on the internet under Carl Gustav Jung, the founder of analytical psychology. Several articles referencing Jung and his research on numbers came up. Most of it is contained in his "Collected Works."[9] Later, as I read from the "Collected Works," Jung regarded numbers as archetypes of order and mythological entities and, as such, are not inventions of the conscious mind but are spontaneous products of the unconscious.[10] He recognized that numbers are symbolic clues that aid in coming to consciousness. Through his study of his patient's dreams, Jung came to believe that the smaller numbers (1 through 9) are consistently symbols of personified collective traits. Because the numbers 1 to 4 occur with the greatest frequency, Jung speculated that these numbers were the most primitive archetype of order in the human mind with the first 4 numbers in particular symbolizing different phases of the journey of the self, different expressions of transformation. The number 1, symbolized by the circle, denotes the unity with self and God. Two is associated with opposites, e.g. good and bad, dark and light, yin and yang, etc. The number 3 denotes a transcendent quality that leads to 4, the symbol of wholeness. Jung felt that "numbers not only express order, they create it. That is why they generally appear in times of psychic disorientation in order to compensate a chaotic state."[11] Furthermore, numbers possess a numinous quality that can link us to something larger than ourselves – The Divine, the Universe, a cosmic truth.

This was revelatory! I was now a year into the Dream Leadership program and no one had discussed or presented numbers as **archetypes.** Yet numbers inhabited my dreams with regularity as well as the dreams of friends and classmates. But their relevance to the meaning of the dream was not apparent. For me this was a gaping hole and I wanted to understand more. What does it mean to the everyday person that numbers are archetypes?

Archetypes Defined

An archetype is not your everyday word or concept. The term "archetype" has its origins in ancient Greek. The root words are **_archein_,** which means old or original and **_typos_,**[12] which means model, pattern or type. Essentially an archetype is the original pattern or model from which copies are made. For example, in literature Hercules or Athena is the model, or archetype for the hero figure. In the Judeo-Christian religions, the archetypes for faith include Abraham, Moses, Isaiah, and Mary.

An archetype is a universal symbol, character or theme that is common and recurring across cultures or throughout history. Carl Jung used the concept of archetype in his theory of the human psyche. He believed that archetypes reside within the mind's "collective unconscious" of people all over the world.[13]

The term "collective unconscious" was coined by Jung and refers to ancestral memory and experience common to all people and is distinct from the individual's unconscious. These archetypes may not necessarily be explained by anything in a person's own life but their meaning seems innate. Freud called these "archaic remnants."[14] Jung gave the example of snake dreams, which are very common even among city-dwellers who may have never seen a snake. These experiences go beyond the individual's mind. How does this play out in our own dreams? We all know the sensation of falling from a tree, a ledge or a building while we may not actually experienced such a fall. This experience is a common dream situation regardless of age, sex or culture. In other words, it is archetypal.

Jung studied extensively myths and art from across cultures to build his concept of archetypes. He argued that the collective unconscious has a profound influence on our lives. While he believed that archetypes are inherited and innate, the form they take in our dreams and fantasies are individualized and depend upon our own cultural references. For example, the trickster archetype is someone who disobeys rules and conventional behavior. He or she is the con man/woman. In our culture, examples include Rumpelstiltskin in the Brothers Grimm's Children's and the Household Tales, Jack Sparrow in Walt Disney's Pirates of the Caribbean, and the Joker in the Batman comics and movie. Some indigenous examples include Loki, the shape shifting giant in Norse mythology;

coyotes to the Native Americans, and Anansi, the spider trickster of Africa. Archetypes represent or express common human needs, instincts and potential. The ancients and indigenous peoples called these personal archetypes Spirit Guides or Allies.

Mother Archetype

One of the primary archetypes is the Mother. Motherhood is as old as life. We would not have survived without a connection to a nurturing one when we were a young infant. We come into the world instinctively knowing how to suckle at her breast. The mother as nurturer is one of the best attributes of this archetype especially as it relates to caring and selflessness. Other symbols of this archetype include the Virgin Mary, Mother Earth, Eve, and the Great Mother deities such as Gaia and Cybele.[15]

All archetypes also have a negative, dark, or shadow side. In the example of the Mother, she is also the woman who abandons her child. To Jung, the symbols of mother represent not simply our relationship with her, but also how she influences our own growth, our move toward independence and mature love.[16] The familiar fairytale, Cinderella contains the two mother archetypes, the good mother or fairy godmother and her shadow, the wicked stepmother. The wicked stepmother represents the mother who does not nurture the child. She is not the rightful mother. The fairy godmother, in contrast, is the projection of a more caring figure.

Jung believed that the mother archetype, like many other archetypes, exists within us from infancy. Furthermore, babies project their own motherly ideals onto the person they feel is their primary nurturer. This can be a grandmother, nanny, teacher or anyone the child sees as providing the majority of his or her care.[17]

Regardless of culture, the foremost symbol for the ancient Earth Mother goddess is the 4 sided square. It is associated with the solid earth from which substance, mass, volume, strength and stability arises. Four is inseparably connected with order in the world. Not only do we organize space on the ground by the 4 cardinal directions – north, south, east and west—but we also organize time by dividing the year into 4 seasons.

Father Archetype

The male counterpart is the Father archetype. Besides our own fathers, dream images of the father include God, a god, a giant, a devil, an older wise man, leader, the sun, a holy man, a dominating boss, judge, a hero, etc. Our father is the most important figure of original authority and strength in our lives - or lack of it. As with any archetype, both light and dark aspects exist. A positive father guides and protects those under his care. The positive qualities of the Father principle include order, discipline, rationality, achievement, organization, self-reliance, authority and inspiration. This is traditionally associated with the number 1.

When our inner authority figure is supportive, our dreams include capable, benevolent and helpful kings, healers, guides, and heroes. Examples of the light side of the father are Gregory Peck in "To Kill a Mockingbird" and Mufasa, the father figure to Simba in Disney's "The Lion King." The dark or shadow Father emerges when the caring protection and guidance turns into rigidity, control and coldness. Examples of the dark side of the father include Darth Vader in "Star Wars" and James Gandolfini in "The Sopranos."[18]

Each type of archetype has its own set of values, meaning and personality traits. They help us gain insights into our own emotions, behaviors, and motivations.

Animal Archetypes

Animal symbols characterize our nations, our sports teams, and our schools and colleges. Animals also serve as archetypes in dreams. Animal symbols date back to the earliest cave drawings. Animals were revered and, in some cases, worshiped. Each animal symbolizes something in terms of its strength and its weakness. They point to our instinctual nature and the need to integrate that part of ourselves with our conscious self.

For example, terrestrial animals often relate to power that must be controlled, overcome or re-expressed. Birds are considered symbols of the soul while aquatic life points to the inner awareness, intuition, creative imagination, and development. A wonderful book to read and use as a reference is *Animal Speak* by Ted Andrews. It is a detailed guide to the spiritual and magical powers of many of the earth's creatures.

Numbers Vibrate

Just as animals, people, and nature are archetypes, so are numbers. They have meaning beyond their symbol. But what is the source of their metaphysical meaning? The answer invariably leads back to Pythagoras, the philosopher and mathematician. We know him from his famous geometry theorem we learned in math class. Yet we know relatively little about his other achievements. Pythagoras founded a philosophical and religious school based upon his beliefs. One of his beliefs was that numbers possess mystical meaning. Each number had its own personality – masculine or feminine, perfect or incomplete, beautiful or ugly.[19]

The centerpiece of Pythagorean thought is the idea of order: musical, social, and mathematical order, the order of the cosmos, and ethical and social order. The order can be expressed in numbers. Thus numbers became a connector between the Divine and the created world. This gave rise to the idea that numbers have vibration. This observation stemmed from Pythagoras noticing that the intervals of the musical scale correspond to the relative lengths of the vibrating strings, which he expressed by the ratios 1:2, 2:3, and 3:4. The underlying premise of Pythagoras' numerology was that every number has a vibration. This was a very unique view back then. Today we know that everything in the universe is made of energy. What differentiates one form of energy from another is the speed at which it vibrates. For example, light vibrates at a very high frequency, while a rock vibrates at a lower frequency. People vibrate at different frequencies. Our thoughts and feelings can affect the frequency at which we vibrate, which in turn can attract us to energy moving at a similar frequency. Don't we all know someone who is very vibrant?

Numerology

At Pythagoras' school, courses in self-development included a semester on the "Science of Numbers" more commonly known as Numerology today. Numerology is derived from the Latin word *'numerus'* for number and the Greek word *'logos'* for meaning, thought and word. Numerology is the study of the mystical relationship between a number and coinciding events. Using numerology, you can discover a person's strengths and weaknesses, deep inner needs, talents, and ways of dealing with others. You can find out the best times to marry, change jobs, move, etc. Using birthdates and names, a number is derived which represents possible awareness, experience, talents and characteristics.

Dreams do not require you to know numerology to understand them. What is most important is your own intuition about the meaning of the number or any other symbol. Just like the other symbols in dreams, we need to use our inner-wisdom when interpreting the meaning of numbers. They are as unique as you are.

Is there a particular number that you have an affinity with or that your body reacts to? Do you feel goose bumps or a slight tingle when you sit in a seat or row with a certain number or hear the number called? Do you have a sense of color with a certain number? If so, don't dismiss this. You may be naturally tapping into something with roots that stretch back to ancient times.

CHAPTER 3

WAYS NUMBERS MIGHT APPEAR IN DREAMS

Just like the other symbols, numbers appear in our dreams in a variety of ways. Sometimes they appear literally - you see the number 6 floating in front of you. Other times the number may be less obvious. Your dream might include 5 swans, or 3 purses, etc. What is important is that you notice them; that you are open to their presence in your dreams. Until I started researching numbers as archetypes, I did not focus on the quantities of things in my dreams. By overlooking this, I missed an important dimension of the dream's meaning.

Let's explore a few of the ways numbers appear in dreams.

Stand-alone or Series

Numbers may appear as a single number or in a series of numbers, which can be strings of large numbers. For example, they may appear as floating literally in space or standing in the middle of a field or you might see a number on a door or on a sign, and sometimes a person in your dream may even speak the number. The point is that the number appears directly and prominently as itself. There is no overlooking the fact that it is a number.

A friend of mine dreamed of the number 1,000,230,000 floating in space. What is the significance of this large number? In instances of a large number it is helpful to break it down to its simplest number. What do I mean? Add all the digits together like this – $1+0+0+0+2+3+0+0+0+0 = 6$. (Numerology does this with birth-dates and names. You add the month, day and year together and reduce it to its lowest number.) This can be done regardless of the size of the number. You could then explore what the resulting number may mean in the dream.

Julie, a client of mine, has had the number 34 appear several times in her dreams. I suggested that she investigate the meaning of the numbers, the 3 and 4, separately. Then add the numbers together, 3+4=7 and look at the meaning of the single digit 7.

Indirectly

Sometimes the appearance of numbers is less obvious. You do not see a specific number per se; rather you become aware that there a specific number of characters or objects in the dream, e.g., your dream includes 3 kittens, 5 children, or 2 purses.

In one of my own dreams, I observed 7 wooden coffins lying on the shore that then were pushed into a lake. At first this was a disturbing image to me. Why coffins? I was not focused on the number of coffins just their presence. But thanks to my research, I discovered how important the number 7 was to my dream. In Numerology, 7 is closely associated with spiritual enlightenment and awakening. Fear gave way to excitement about what the number was pointing to in my dream. It was validating what was happening in my waking life. I was about to begin the Dream Leadership program at The Haden Institute, which was transformative. It is noteworthy too, that my dream did not show 3 coffins or 5 coffins which would have offered a different meaning than the number 7.

Age/Markers in Time

In working with dreams, I invariably ask the dreamer the age of the people in the dream. Sometimes the age of a person is a marker for a certain time in the dreamer's life. For example, a baby appeared in Tom's dream. I asked him the age of the baby. He did not hesitate to say 5. He has no grandchildren, or children of his own. I asked him what happened 5 years ago or 5 months ago that was significant. He thought a minute and then his eyes got bigger. Indeed something very traumatic had happened to him 5 years ago. The number allowed him to get in touch with a deeper meaning of his dream.

A number may appear on a door or you may get off the elevator on a certain floor, like the 18th floor. The dream may be pointing to something in your life that happened 18 years ago or something that shifted deep within you unconsciously. 18 years ago. The point here is that this can be a very productive way of exploring an aspect of your dream.

Dates

A number in a dream may represent a date such as an anniversary or birthday. In this way the number may serve as a time-keeper and give clues to events that took place during your waking life.

Lucky Numbers

If you have a lucky number it may show up in your dream. When that happens, your unconscious mind may be helping you to make a major decision or life choice.

Addresses

The number in your dream may be the number of your house and it may draw you to a memory that is associated with that house. David's recent dream had him returning to his home address of his youth, 311 Adams Avenue. Was the dream pointing to the past? Was it showing him the child he was then or issues that he faced when he lived there? Regardless, the address points to a place associated with deep feelings. Is it something that he still needs to assimilate into his current life? Or could this be his unconscious wanting him to "address" a problem in his life?

Shapes

Sometimes numbers are expressed symbolically as a shape, such as a square, rectangle, triangle or circle. These shapes can be associated specifically with numbers; the square and rectangle are 4 sided and therefore associated with the number 4; the triangle with the number 3, and the circle with the number 1.

A recent dream of mine took place in a large church that was in the shape of an octagon, an 8-sided shape. A wedding was being held. In numerology, 8 is a number that points to success and security. For me, the dream was very affirming of what I am trying to achieve in my life as a spiritual director and dream leader.

Money

It is no surprise that dreams with dollar signs and money in them are about value and worth. Money is payment for time or effort. Things of value can be a new talent you deeply desire or a gift within you. Money is ultimately about our attitudes about what matters most to you.

For example, Shelby had the following dream: She is at a wedding reception for her daughter and her son-in-law. She paid $30,000 for the reception. Her new son-in-law's parents were supposed to contribute an equal amount but did not. To have the wedding her daughter wants Shelby has to kick in another $30,000. In the dream Shelby felt that now the $60,000 wedding would be impressive. In the dream, she is aware that this has depleted her savings significantly. She worries about whether there will any left for the other two children.

The two numbers 3 and 6 are significant to the dream. The zeros are there for emphasis. There are many meanings for the number 3 but I believe that this dream is about her gift of creative expression and the value of it. She is trying to integrate this aspect of herself (the wedding symbol) more fully in her life. She doesn't know if she has the energy to pursue this. With the number 6, harmony and union are possible but they will require effort.

Money means many things depending upon what happening in the dream. Losing or finding money, stolen money, poverty and wealth all are about symbols of energy, self-worth, and confidence. As in all dreams, context is crucial to their meaning and wisdom of the dreams. Just like the other symbols in dreams, we need to use our intuition, creativity and inner-wisdom to explore their meaning. The following chapters will take you deeper into the language of numbers.

CHAPTER 4

YOUR OWN WISDOM

Up to this point the focus of the book has been on the history of the wisdom of numbers and the importance they play in the meaning of our dreams and waking life. But what about our own wisdom? What personal connection do we have to a number?

Here is the space and opportunity to connect to your own inner wisdom about a number in your dream or a number that you have noticed in your waking life.

To begin, gather some art supplies you would like to use like magic markers, paints, pastels, watercolors, charcoal, or colored pencils. Don't forget paper.

You may want to use the circle at the end of this chapter as a guide. It is a mandala (Sanskrit for circle or wholeness). Mandalas have a long history and are found throughout the world. They are used in a variety of ways – communication, art therapy, meditation, healing and contemplation. Why do people of all cultures since ancient times find a circle such a meaningful form for expression? I believe Carl Jung provides some insight when he said that "it is a representation of the unconscious self, the wholeness of the personality, which if all goes well is harmonious…"[20] As Suzanee Fincher says in her book, *Creating Mandalas,* as it was with Jung, so it is with you… Your mandalas reveal the dynamics of the Self as it creates a matrix where your unique identity unfolds."

You can use the mandala or a blank piece of paper. There are not rules or constrictions with regard to materials used. Your instinct and feelings should inspire and guide you. It is not about the final product… it's about the journey. Regardless, you will have a representation of something meaningful and personal.

Pick a place and time when there are few distractions so you can close your eyes and be present to this exercise.

Sit comfortably with the clean, blank paper or mandala in front of you. You may want to light a candle to help center yourself.

If possible, have someone read the following to you. If no one is around, then read the following slowly out aloud to yourself. Allow the words to settle so your imagination can engage them freely:

Meditation exercise

I would like you to sit comfortably. Close your eyes. Relax your body. Maybe take a couple of breaths in and release out with a big sigh. Become aware of your breath. Be present.

Now, look at your number from your dream or the number that you have awareness of in waking life. What does it look like? Does it have color? Size, a shape? What type of energy does it have? Is it soft, undulating? Or jagged, loud, sharp.
Is it vibrating?
Is it masculine, feminine, both or neither?
Do you sense a feeling or emotion that comes up inside of you with the number?
Does it have an odor? Taste? How does it feel to the touch? Does it have a sound?
Does it have weight? If so, is it heavy? Or light as a feather?
Do you like it?
Are there any qualities that you associate with it?
Does it have a purpose?

Be with the number.

After a few minutes open your eyes. Now take the sheet of paper in front of you and record with words or images whatever came to you. Don't judge this. Don't over think this. Allow yourself to just go with whatever comes to mind. Let it be. Let it flow into your consciousness. You are connecting raw material. The meaning of it will become clearer later as you go through this book.

Whenever a word or image comes up, try different associations to that word or image. Allow your feelings and emotions inspire you. Record or draw it. Keep at it until you feel you have exhausted that avenue of thought or feeling.

If we are going to tap into our inner wisdom this exercise and these questions are not so farfetched. As I have shown earlier in the book, human life has an intimate connection with numbers. We just have to tap into it. So give yourself permission to do that.

Once you are finished, set what you recorded aside. Keep it handy after you have read the chapter on your particular number.

What's Next

The following chapters provide information on the metaphysical and cultural meaning of each number. They are to be used as a guide in exploring possible meanings of numbers in your dreams and/or waking lives.

After reading about any given number, go back to your own drawing. Do you see any similarities? Does it capture the general attributes associated with the number? Does it give you additional insights to the meaning of your dream?

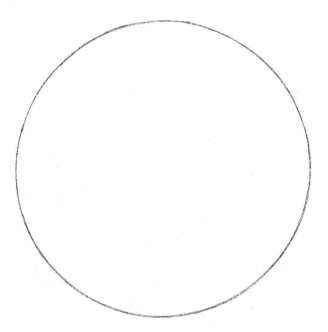

The following chapters provide details on some of the metaphysical, archetypal, and cultural meanings of the numbers 1-9 plus the master numbers and zero. It is not by any means a comprehensive gathering of information on each number. It is intended to give you a flavor of the spiritual meaning of the number from ancient times as well as common cultural uses and expressions of the number.

CHAPTER 5

THE NUMBER 1

The meaning of each number is complex. Not only does it have personal meaning to you but it also has mystical and archetypal wisdom that is reflected throughout the world and can also inhabit our dreams. Let me get you started with a few examples:

- In most cultures, number 1 is synonymous with being the best, the leader, the winner, and the person regarded as most worthy of our respect.

- Our language includes expressions like "taking care of number 1" and "the 1 and only." However, not all expressions are self-directed. When someone is calm and wise, he/she is "at 1 with his/herself" or the universe.

- This number wisdom was formalized by the Pythagoreans who believed the number 1 as the 'monad' or "oneness." The monad reflects The First, The Essence and more dramatically, The Immutable Truth. It is the number from which all things begin. They viewed the number 1 as a male vibration, focusing on energy outward and as having traditional masculine attributes: organization, achievement, strength, tenacity, self-reliance.

In numerology, the number 1 is a powerful force that produces results and does not allow anything or anyone to limit its potential. The 1 is aggressive, a necessary energy for creating and producing. The 1 is always leading others. The 1 is a pragmatist, at times ruthless, and independent to a fault. It is self-determined and self-sufficient. It is the most individualist of all numbers.

The number 1, like its shape, reflects its meaning: it walks upright with purpose and pride.

In dream work… when 1 appears in a dream as either a single digit or repeatedly in a sequence like 1,11,111,1111, etc., it is a reminder that we are all connected.

1 is a strong, assertive symbol of individuality, autonomy, originality, and the beginning of self-discovery and self-empowerment.

Number 1 points to new beginnings, creation, independence, uniqueness, striving forward, ambition and will power. It also resonates with initiative, instinct and intuition.

Number 1 encourages us to step out of our comfort zone. It tells us that we create our own reality with our thoughts, beliefs and actions. It may be suggesting a need to develop your individuality and creativity or to grow spiritually.

KEY QUALITIES: *INDIVIDUALITY*
                     INDEPENDENCE
                     SELF-ASSURED
                     BEGINNINGS
                     UNITY

Negative or Shadow Meaning

The negative side of number 1 is self-doubt, low self-esteem, or selfishness. The number may imply that the dreamer only cares about her/himself and needs to consider the feelings of others. It points to intolerance, narrow-mindedness, stubbornness, impatience, arrogance and dominance. It may signify loneliness.

Your Meaning

Now go to your dream. Given what you have read here about the possible meanings of the number 1, jot down your thoughts or draw images of how this number may influence the meaning of your dream. Feel free to use the mandala on page 37 at the end of Chapter 4.

CHAPTER 6

THE NUMBER 2

Here are some examples of the meaning of the number 2:

Duality

There are two sides to every coin

Yin yang

Left and right, front and back, up and down, day and night

Good and evil, male and female, etc.

Pythagoras believed that the number 2 was female. (He believed that even numbers are female; odd numbers are male.)

The notion of twoness was called the Dyad by the Greek philosophers and referred to the principle of polarity. The Dyad simultaneously divides and unites, repels and attracts, separates from unity and craves return to it. Linguistically, this is reflected in words beginning with *bi* (unity) and *di* (separation).

The number 2 generally signifies balance, partnership, diversity, conflict and polarity.

In numerology, 2s are sensitive, tactful, diplomatic and cooperative. 2s tend to be peacemakers and are studious and patient. It also is the number which reflects your Divine life purpose or soul mission. Number 2s desire harmony.

In dream work….. 2s indicate choice and balance. Their presence may be telling you to make a decision you may be putting off.

2s may point to a current conflict in your life.

A 2 may point to a need to bring balance to your efforts, budgets, time, etc.

It may be pointing to partnerships and the family, friend and romantic relationships of the dreamer.

Repeating 2s in a dream may indicate new ideas and concepts that are beginning to take shape.

Key Qualities: OPPOSITES/DUALITY
                  COOPERATION/PARTNERSHIP
                  CONFLICT/POLARITY
                  SERVICE TO OTHERS

Shadow Meaning

Depending upon the context of the dream, the number 2 may suggest a conflict with another, weakness and/or indecision about something important in your waking life.

It may point to being too dependent, manipulative and passive-aggressive. Can be lazy, careless and overly-sensitive.

Your Meaning

Now go to your dream. Given what you have read here about the possible meanings of the number 2, jot down your thoughts or draw images of how this number may influence the meaning of your dream. Feel free to use the mandala on page 37.

CHAPTER 7

THE NUMBER 3

There seems to be an inherent trinary nature to the world; heaven, earth and waters and the human as body, mind and spirit.

Neurologically, we are programmed to remember things in threes.

Tic tac toe
Winston Churchill's "blood, sweat and tears"
U.S.A.
Snap, crackle and pop
Past, present and future
Beginning, middle and end
3 square meals a day

How about expressions like the third time's the charm?

In fairy tales, heroes/heroines are often given 3 tests. They overcome the challenges on the third try. Genies grant 3 wishes.

3 wise men
3 musketeers
3 cheers - not two; not four!

The examples are virtually limitless. Can you think of any?

- The number 3 moves forward, from overcoming duality (number 2) to synthesis. Just like the third leg of a stool, the number 3 points to balance. It also may connote growth and creative power.

- With the number 3, divine aspects of mind, body and spirit come into awareness.

- 3 is the number of the universal triangle, the Trinity.

In numerology, the number 3 is very creative. It may also suggest a strong need to express feelings, ideas and visions of the imagination coupled with an extroverted personality. They tend to be tolerant, inspiring, youthful and dynamic.

In dreams, a 3 almost always points to creative self-expression.

It may be a message that your true goals or visions are coming to fruition; that all things are possible and attainable.

3s, or a series of threes, appearing in your dream indicates self-discipline through service to others.

It manifests abundance, productivity and unity.

If you are dreaming about a relationship and 3 shows up, be aware of a triangle.

It is also a sign of possible pregnancy.

Key Qualities: CREATIVITY
SACRED TRINITY
EXPANSION/GROWTH
OPTIMISM/ENTHUSIASM

Shadow Meaning

The number 3 may be a sign of problems with communicating and blocked or scattered energies. It may imply the separation from reality or a lack of grounding. It may point to impatience, vanity, and superficiality.

Extravagant, scattered and superficial.

Your Meaning

Now go to your dream. Given what you have read here about the possible meaning of the number 3, jot down your thoughts or draw images of how this number may influence the meaning of your dream. Feel free to use the mandala on page 37.

CHAPTER 8

THE NUMBER 4

The Pythagoreans believed that the number 4, the Tetrad, was a perfect number and taught that it symbolized God. They saw 4 parts to the soul: mind, opinion, science, and sense.

The number 4 is symbolized by the square and serves as the basis of order for many natural things:

4 phases of the moon – crescent, waxing, full and waning
4 directions – north, south, east and west
4 leaf clover
4 winds of the Bible
4 seasons – winter, spring, summer and fall
4 elements – earth, air, fire and water
4 letters of the sacred name of God, YHWY
4 Rivers to Paradise that form a cross (the Garden of Eden was said to be within the four rivers)
4 psychic functions: sensing, thinking, feeling and intuition
Alchemic processes: hot, cold, wet and dry

C.G. Jung saw the squaring of the circle – a mandala (from the Hindi for circle or center) as a way to understand the self and represent a unified concept or archetype of wholeness. He created many beautiful and haunting dream images using the mandala.

Most of our structures are built around 4-sided shapes – square or rectangle. They are symbols of strength and stability.

In numerology, the number 4 is about strength, stability, dependability and productivity. 4s believe in effort and control. For 4s it is all about orderliness, practicality and organizing.

In dream work…the number 4 appearing in your dream may be an indication that you are being guided and supported in your endeavors. Trust that your hard work and efforts will bring well-earned rewards.

4 is an indication that all is as it should be.

Key Qualities: TRUSTWORTHY
                 SOLID/STABLE
                 ORDERLY
                 FOUNDATIONAL

Shadow Meaning

The contra meaning in a dream suggests limitations, narrowness and restrictions. Take note of any feelings of inflexibility or of holding yourself back. For example, you may not be giving yourself enough credit for a situation or you may be hindering yourself in the attainment of your goals. It may suggest dullness and indecision.

Your Meaning

Now go to your dream. Given what you have read here about the possible meanings of the number 4, jot down your thoughts or draw images of how this number may influence the meaning of your dream. Feel free to use the mandala on page 37.

CHAPTER 9

THE NUMBER 5

One of the first things we think about when we hear or see the number 5 is our 5 senses – sight, sound, smell, hearing and touch. This is the case except in Eastern cultures where there are 6 – the extra being the mind.

5 fingers of the human hand
5 vowels in the English alphabet
"High 5" is a social gesture of celebrating
5 continents – Africa, Antarctica, Asia, North and South America
5 Great Lakes – Erie, Huron, Ontario, Michigan and Superior

The Hamsa (means 5) hand or amulet is very common in the Middle East. It is used by Jews and Muslims as magical protection against the evil eye. It is often worn by peace activists in the Middle East.

The Pentagram or 5 pointed star depicts individuality and spiritual aspiration and education when it is pointed upward. (Pointed downward represents witchcraft.)

5 is an ordering principle for books and words of wisdom
5 commandments for lay people in Buddhism
The 5 main intellectual virtues mentioned by Aristotle
(intellect, scientific knowledge, skill, practical wisdom and wisdom)
The 5 Books of Moses, The Pentateuch.

The Pythagoreans thought of 5 as "hieros gamos", the marriage between heaven and earth.

5 is the center of the soul or feeling plane. It is a spiritual number representing love and freedom of expression. 5s are idea people with a love of variety and the ability to adapt to most situations.

In numerology, 5s are likely to be restless, lively, adventuresome, and quick-thinking. They tend to be versatile, courageous, flexible and quick-thinking.

In dream work 5s appearing in dreams suggests energy, change, impulsiveness, a free soul, self-emancipation and curiosity.

5s appearing in a dream may be a premonition of important discoveries, adventures or actions to be taken in waking life.

It may be time to break free from the old constraints that have been holding you back. It is time to live your life with passion and purpose.

KEY QUALITIES: CHANGE/EXPANSION
                      FREEDOM LOVING
                      ADAPTABLE/TRAVEL
                      CURIOUS
                      NEWNESS

Shadow Meaning

Depending upon the dream, 5s may suggest a lack of focus and a materialistic outlook on life. 5s may also be pointing to over-indulgence, addictive and compulsive behaviors that need to be addressed. 5s can be unstable, careless, and chaotic.

Your Meaning

Now go to your dream. Given what you have read here about the possible meanings of the number 5, jot down your thoughts or draw images of how this number may influence the meaning of your dream. Feel free to use the mandala on page 37.

CHAPTER 10

THE NUMBER 6

According to the ancients, 6 is the most perfect number as it is both the sum and the product of its parts: it is formed by adding 1 + 2 + 3 or by multiplying 1 x 2 x 3.

Snowflakes are 6 sided

6 occurs widely in crystalline structures such as quartz and graphite

Insects creep and crawl on 6 legs

Honey bees instinctively create a 6-sided honey comb

The well-known 3-4-5 Pythagorean triangle has an area and a semiperimeter of 6

There are 6 directions: forward, backward, left, right, up and down

6 is the symbol of luck, the highest number on a single dice

"The sixth sense" refers to extra sensory perception (ESP)

The standard guitar has 6 strings

Creation occurred in 6 days according to the Hebrew Bible.

In numerology 6 is considered the most harmonious of the single digit numbers. The most important influence of the 6 is its loving and caring nature. Properly named the maternal number, it is all about sacrificing, caring, healing, protecting, and teaching others. It resonates with cooperation, union, love, home, family and domesticity, and the monetary aspects of life. 6s are the glue that keeps the family or community together. Having a strong sense of responsibility, 6s can be counted on to do their fair share.

In dream work... 6 may indicate domestic or self-harmony, meeting responsibilities, love and abundance.

It may imply "new love" will enter your life.

Dreaming of 6 may be a message that your material and monetary needs will be meet.

It may also point to forgiveness and compassion and the need to go within to find both.

KEY QUALITIES: LOVE/FAMILY/NURTURE
MATERIAL ABUNDANCE
COMPASSION
BALANCE/RESPONSIBILITY

Shadow Meaning

The number 6 in a dream, depending upon its context, may point to difficulty in accepting love and support. It may suggest you have nothing else to give, a depletion of feelings. It may also suggest smugness and a self-satisfied attitude. 6 may point to anxiety, worry, and jealousy.

Your Meaning

Now go to your dream. Given what you have read here about the possible meanings of the number 6, jot down your thoughts or draw images of how this number may influence the meaning of your dream. Feel free to use the mandala on page 37.

CHAPTER 11

THE NUMBER 7

Pick an odd number between 1 and 10 and chances are it will be 7. Whatever your creed or culture the number 7 is important and special and the number most chosen by people.

We have an affinity with 7.[21] When it comes to feeling lucky or seeking the power of the divine nothing beats the power of 7.

If you google the number 7 you will get millions of hits on its biblical, magical, and cultural importance. The fundamental rhythm of our lives is part of the cycle of 7 days of the week. Here are a few other examples:

7

Colors in a rainbow

Notes to the scale

Wonders of the world

Oceans

Deadly sins and virtues

The number of Chakras

Snow White and the 7 dwarfs

7 Brides for 7 Brothers

7 ages of man (Shakespeare)

7 is the optimum number of hours of sleep

Babylonian ziggurats were built with 7 storeys, the Egyptians spoke of 7 gates of the netherworld, the Vedic sun god had 7 horses, and Muslims must walk around the Kaaba 7 times during the Hajj. The birth mother of the Buddha's mother died of joy 7 days after giving birth.

The number 7 is one of the most significant numbers in the Bible. God created the world in 6 days and rested on the 7th. The number 7 appears more than 700 times throughout the Bible. Solomon took 7 years to build his temple, Job had 7 sons and the great flood came 7 days after Noah went into the ark. Christ spoke 7 words from the cross.

David and Victoria Beckham named their daughter Harper Seven after Harper Lee, the author of *To Kill a Mockingbird*, Victoria's favorite book. They also chose Seven because it symbolizes spiritual perfection.

In numerology, 7 symbolizes humanity's deep inner-need to find depth and spiritual connection. It resonates with energies of faith and spirituality: spiritual awakening and awareness, enlightenment, mysticism, intuition, and inner-knowing. It is the number of perfection, security and healing. 7s are analytical, focused, contemplative, refined and gracious. It is the teaching and learning number.

In dream work…the mystical number 7 speaks of our inner-selves and inner-wisdom, birth and rebirth, solitude, spiritual awakening and enlightenment.

It also suggests healing and intuition. The number can be an indication that you are on the Divine path that is right for you. Keep up the good work that you are doing and positive things will flow into your life.

Dreams with the number 7 points to beneficial times to come, obstacles overcome and success realized.

KEY QUALITIES: MYSTICAL/INNER WISDOM
                          TRANSFORMATION
                          INTUITION
                          HEALING

Shadow Meaning

Depending on the dream's context, 7 may also tell of feelings of being misunderstood by others, isolation and separateness, and difficulty in maintaining relationships.

It can point to inactivity, stagnation, narrowness and an unwillingness to share ideas.

Your Meaning

Now go to your dream. Given what you have read here about the possible meanings of the number 7, jot down your thoughts or draw images of how this number may influence the meaning of your dream. Feel free to use the mandala on page 37.

CHAPTER 12

THE NUMBER 8

In China, the number 8 is highly esteemed. It is a homonym for prosperity. The opening ceremony of the Summer Olympics in China began on 8/8/08 at 8 minutes past 8:00 pm.

In the Sermon on the Mount, Christ mentions 8 beatitudes. It seems that the eightfold division of the path that leads to eternal bliss is a universal concept. Just as the Buddha teaches the noble eightfold path leading to cosmic equilibrium, the basic rules for the aspiring Sufi in Islam are also expressed in the 8 sentences of the Path of Junayd.

On a less spiritual plane, there are:

Stop signs are octagonal in shape
Spiders have 8 legs, so do octopi
8 fluid ounces in a cup; 8 pints in a gallon
The mathematical symbol for infinity is an 8 on the its side
The amount of cloud cover in the sky is measured in
oktas (from 0 to 8)

The Pythagoreans called the number 8 the "Ogdoad" and considered it the "little holy number".

In numerology, the number 8 resonates with the vibrations of personal power, self-confidence, executive ability, harmony and balance. It carries the energies of success and material wealth. 8s tend to value control and the ability to make decisions. 8 is about reaping rewards, attracting your desires and personal improvement.

In dream work… 8 suggests that goals are coming to fruition. It may imply an auspicious offer or windfall may be coming your way.

When 8 appears in your dreams it may be time to trust your intuition and instincts and take appropriate action.

Repeating 8s may be a message to keep your finances in check to ensure a solid foundation for yourself and your family.

KEY QUALITIES: INFINITE/ETERNITY/SYMMMETRY
                   ENERGIES OF SUCCESS
                   ABUNDANCE
                   PRACTICAL
                   STRONG

Shadow Meaning

Depending upon the context of the dream, 8 may suggest someone who is overbearing and bossy; someone who can alienate partners and fall short of creating a tolerant and romantic atmosphere. It also can point to greed.

Your Meaning

Now go to your dream. Given what you have read here about the possible meanings of the number 8, jot down your thoughts or draw images of how this number may influence the meaning of your dream. Feel free to use the mandala on page 37.

CHAPTER 13

THE NUMBER 9

Because 9 is composed of the powerful 3 x 3, it is called the Triple Triad and points to completion, fulfillment, attainment and beginnings.

9 is a celestial number of order and many ancient traditions speak of 9 worlds, spheres, or levels of being and awareness.

Cats have 9 lives
'Dress to the 9s'
Overjoyed? You are on cloud 9
A numerological cycle is a 9 year cycle
There are 9 months to human pregnancy

The Pythagoreans called the number 9 the Ennead and saw 9 as unlucky as it was one short of 10, which they considered perfect. They saw 9 stages for our advancing from a lower stage to a higher more evolved stage of life.

In numerology, 9s is the number of Universal love, eternity, faith, karma, spiritual awareness and enlightenment, and service to humanity. 9s are achievers, possessing high ideals and great ideas.

9 is the number of cosmic consciousness; awakening of the higher self to the alignment of all that is, was and ever will be.

9 is a humanitarian number and indicates service to others, completions and endings, leadership, inspiration, closure, and living as a positive example to others to follow.

In dream work…seeing a 9 in your dream, which is more unusual than the other numbers, may be a prompt to get on with your Divine Life purpose.

As number 9 represents ending and completions, one of its messages is that all things must come to an end in order for new beginnings to happen.

9 appearing in a dream may indicate that the dreamer is spiritually advanced and should follow their life path and soul purpose.

Dreaming of 9 may mean that it is time to put your natural skills, talents and abilities to good use in serving humanity. Shine your light brightly for the benefit of yourself and others.

9 in a dream may indicate a situation or relationship that is no longer serving you well, drawing to an end.

KEY QUALITIES: HUMANITARIAN
                          ENDING/CLOSURE
                          SPIRITUAL AWAKENING
                          INSPIRATION

Shadow Meaning

If expressed negatively, 9 may indicate being ego-centric, unsympathetic, intolerant and/or possessive of others and their ideas and values. It may also point to being financially careless, moody, bullying, overly emotional, sullen and restless.

Your Meaning

Now go to your dream. Given what you have read here about the possible meanings of the number 9, jot down your thoughts or draw images of how this number may influence the interpretation of your dream. Feel free to use the mandala on page 37.

CHAPTER 14

THE NUMBER 10 & ZERO

In this chapter, I have combined the numbers 10 and 0 because they are related. In numerology, zero is a symbol rather than a number. In Mathematics, the zero by itself has no attributes, no character traits and is thus valueless by definition. It does, however, have the ability to enhance the qualities of any other single–digit number 1-9. The 10 becomes a higher octave to 1, the 20 raises the qualities of the 2, and so forth.

Early western civilization questioned the importance of the number zero and abstained from using it. But the perception changed with the Neo-Platonist philosophers who expounded the origin and mysticism of the number 0. The origin of 0 can be traced to early Indian civilization. The Sanskrit word *Shunya* means void or nothingness.

The current European system is an adaptation of this system.

The number 0 is a spiritual metaphor for The One, The Supreme Being, or the one without beginning or end. From the womb of the void (0) comes the creative power (1), the source of all life. From 1, the number 2 is born and so on. So 0 does not equate to material nothingness.

In numerology there are 10 numbers plus master numbers. Number 1 signifies the first dawn of existence and 10 is a metaphor for the merging of the individual soul to the ultimate reality.

10 represents synergy, the whole that is greater than the sum of its parts, beyond the number itself.

To the Pythagoreans, 10 was the "perfect number" symbolizing both fulfillment and new beginnings. They called 10 the Decad. The Decad brings all numbers to perfection and completion. With the Decad we are back to the beginning where we started, enriched by the journey.

Something that is exceptional is rated a "perfect 10". It represents the next generation, or a quantum leap ahead. We use the expression "ten times better or ten times worse for emphasis.

In numerology, anyone who has one or more zeros in their birth date has an inherent spirituality which has the potential to help them in understanding the deeper aspects of their life.

So if a 10 or a series of 10s appears in your dream it is suggesting wholeness and perfection.

Your Meaning

Now go to your dream. Given what you have read here about the possible meanings of the number 10, jot down your thoughts or draw images of how this number may influence the interpretation of your dream. Feel free to use the mandala on page 37.

CHAPTER 15

MASTER NUMBERS 11, 22 AND 33

The numbers 11, 22 and 33 are master numbers. Master numbers energetically accentuate the meaning of the single digits. They are considered to be some of the most powerful vibrations known and are thought to symbolize raw potential. The energy that they point to is strong and waiting to be harnessed by those who have the eyes to see.

The fact that 11, 22, and 33 are double-digits numbers consisting of identical single digits is not the reason that they are considered Master numbers. Rather it is that they possess more potential than other numbers. They are highly charged, difficult to handle and require time and effort to integrate their energy into someone's personality.

Master number 11

The number 11 represents instinct and is the most intuitive of all numbers. It points to a connection to your subconscious, to gut feelings and knowledge without rational thought. The 11 is the dreamer. It has all the aspects of the number 2, enhanced and charged with charisma, leadership and inspiration. Individuals connected with the number 11 are extremely powerful and capable of great things, but if not focused on some goal beyond themselves, may find themselves self-sabotaging. The number 11 walks the edge between greatness and self-destruction. The potential for growth, stability and personal power lies in their acceptance of intuitive understanding. For 11 peace is not found in logic but in faith. Many psychics, clairvoyants and prophets are 11s.

Master number 22

The 22 is called the "Master Builder" and is believed to be the most powerful of all numbers. Those associated with the number 22 can turn the most ambitious of dreams into reality. Potentially the most successful of all numbers, it has the inspirational insights of the 11, combined with the practicality and methodical nature of 4. The number 22 points to being unlimited, yet disciplined; having big ideas, big plans coupled with confidence and leadership. Like 11, 22 is capable of greatness, but can apply too much pressure on themselves and shrink from their own ambition, causing internal conflicts.

Master number 33

Known as the "Master Teacher", 33 is the most influential of all numbers. It combines the 11 and the 22 and brings their potential to another level. When fully expressed, 33 lacks all personal ambition and focuses its considerable abilities toward the good of mankind. This number is extremely rare.

Together the three Master numbers represent a triangle of enlightenment:

> The number 11 holds the vision
> The number 22 combines vision with action
> The number 33 offers guidance to the world

It is no wonder that Master numbers can be both a blessing and a curse.

When to reduce these powerful numbers

Generally, when the double-digit number or a date does not have the power to unleash Master number potential, you should reduce it to a single digit. For example, the month of November is the 11th month but it is not a Master number in of itself. However, if you calculate your Life Path and Birth Date number and these numbers appear, then treat them as core numbers and potential Master numbers.

For example, if you were born on September 2, 2001, the date has an 11 in the First Pinnacle of the life cycle or birth date. Here you would acknowledge the Master number. However, when calculating cycles as a whole, then you reduce the Master number to 9+2 = 11 = 2 and 2001 to 3.

This makes sense when you are dealing with cycles as having momentum while a precise date is static.

In numerology only the master numbers 11, 22, and 33 are considered. However, the numbers 44, 55, 66, 77, 88 and 99 may appear to many people throughout their lives, particularly in phases of spiritual growth. For that reason, here is brief recap of their meaning:

44 –Typically means a period of growth through challenge. You are called to pay attention to this challenge and what you think about it. Knowing this allows you to be more proactive instead of merely allowing life to happen to you.

55 – May point to a period of instability and flux that you can master by turning to your higher wisdom and intuition.

66 – Comes up a lot around spiritual awakening or in Yogi theory and/or Kundalini awakenings. It speaks of bringing the sacred to the mundane in life.

77 – Generally points to solitude and turning away from the outer world to establish a deeper connection with one's inner world and the universe as a whole.

88 – Suggests mastery of self-discipline, becoming assertive and challenging authority.

99 – Points to idealism; sees the bigger picture and strives to improve the world. Tendency to be too idealistic which can lead to frustration and disappointment.

Summary

Number	Key Qualities	Shadow Qualities
1	BEGINNINGS SELF-ASSURED INDIVIDUATION INDEPENDENCE UNITY	SELF-DOUBT SELFISHNESS INTOLERANCE LONELINESS
2	DUALITY PARTNERSHIP BALANCE SERVICE TO OTHERS	CONFLICT INDECISION WEAKNESS MANIPULATIVE
3	SACRED TRINITY EXPANSION/.GROWTH CREATIVITY OPTIMISM/ENTHUSIASM	BLOCKED ENERGY UNGROUNDED
4	ORDER STABILITY WHOLENESS FOUNDATIONAL	LIMITATION NARROWNESS INFLEXIBILITY
5	CHANGE/EXPANSION FREEDOM LOVING ADAPTABLE/TRAVEL NEWNESS	UNFOCUSED MATERIALISTIC COMPULSIVE OVERINDULGENT
6	CREATIVITY HARMONY/COOPERATION LOVE/FAMILY/NURTURE BALANCE	DIFFICULTY ACCEPTING LOVE SMUGNESS DEPLETION OF FEELINGS

7	MYSTICAL	MISUNDERSTOOD
	TRANSFORMATION	DIFFICULTY BEING
	INNER WISDOM	ISOLATION
	HEALING	SEPARATENESS
8	INFINITE/ETERNITY	OVERBEARING
	ENERGIES OF SUCCCESS	BOSSY
	ABUNDANCE	PARTY POOPER
	SYMMETRY	
9	HUMANITARIAN	UNSYMPATHETIC
	INSPIRATION	INTOLERANT
	ENDING/CLOSURE	CARELESS
	SPIRITUAL AWAKENING	SULLEN

ZERO

Zero is a symbol rather than a number. The 0 is present in many birth dates and has an important symbolic significance. Philosophically and mathematically, it represents nothing as the numerator and everything as the denominator; the two infinite ends of the finite, neither of which is attainable. Thus it is a mystical symbol, indicative of the degree of spiritual mysticism inherent but rarely developed in the individual. Anyone with one or more zeros in their birth date has an inherent spirituality that they should recognize, for it has the potential to assist them in understanding many of the deeper aspects of life.

Master numbers exist on a higher spiritual plane than the single digits:

ELEVEN

The karmic Master Builder number 11 appears in our dreams indicating self-illumination, intuition and insight. Elevens must work to develop intuition, to tune into psychic forces not available to those with lower numbers.

The 11 is the most intuitive of all numbers.

Elevens in your dreams may be suggesting partnerships, equality and balance. It may also indicate a thirst for spiritual awakening and advancement.

TWENTY-TWO

The 22 is the most powerful of all numbers. The Master Builder number 22 denotes our knowledge, intelligence and mental capacity. The second master number is potentially capable of combining the idealism of the first master number 11, with the ability to put these ideals into a concrete form. When this potential can be realized, the individual becomes a Master Builder, capable of feats beyond all others.

Seeing 22 in your dreams suggests self-mastery and the knowledge of 'all things are possible'. You may need to be more practical and/or goal oriented in your life.

THIRTY-THREE

The 33 is the most influential of all numbers. It is the Master Teacher. When expressed to the fullest, the 33 lacks all personal ambition, and instead focuses its considerable abilities toward the spiritual uplifting of mankind. The karmic Master number 33 appearing in dreams indicates our inner-sanctuary, the spiritual teacher and spiritual wisdom.

CHAPTER 16

CONCLUSION

I have been a dream group leader, dream mentor, and workshop presenter at annual conferences on dreams. I have also worked with all sorts of folks including my favorite – college students with their dreams and art. Even ladies in the hair salon, people at the check-out counter and doctors share their dreams and want to understand them. I cannot tell you how many times someone has said to me "I had the weirdest dream" or "I have this recurring nightmare." In every instance, engaging them in understanding the metaphorical images of their dreams has been met with great appreciation and in many instances relief.

Dreams come to us every night, whether we remember them or not. Scientists are only beginning to understand their value and function. Science is slowly beginning to catch up to what we intuitively know. "Dreams come," as Jeremy Taylor, the preeminent dream guru says, "in the service of healing and wholeness." Time and time again I see how this is true.

This book, which focuses on numbers, represents only one piece of the many images that inhabit our dreams. I hope the contents and tools of this book help you on your journey to understand yourself and your dreams better.

PRACTICAL TIPS – IMPROVING DREAM RECALL

Dreams have tremendous power to transform our lives in so many ways. Working with dreams can help us improve our emotional life, solve difficult waking life challenges, inspire creativity, diagnose possible illnesses, deepen and improve relationships, provide new perspectives and even ideas for new inventions. They can help shape our life purpose.

The good news is that we all dream, every night. The challenge is recalling our dreams. Often when we awake, we vaguely remember having dreamed during the night but we cannot recall any of the dream details. Waking and dreaming memory are not connected as well as they could be. With greater intention, focus, and practice we can change that. Try using the following tips to help increase your dream recall.

1. Set your intention

The single most important step in dream recall is simply deciding that you are truly interested in your dreams and want to remember them. Before you close your eyes to sleep, tell yourself you will remember your dreams.

You may even want to pray to a Dream Guide or Angel to help you recall your dream. If you start with the belief that you can, you will remember your dreams! Trust this.

2. Select a method for recording your dreams

Have you ever woken up from a dream, put on a robe and gone to the kitchen for coffee only to forget your dream? Dreams fade quickly, which is why it is so important to record them.

Most people place journals or a pad of paper and pencil at their bedside. Some people use tape recorders or cell phones to record their recollection of their dreams. Others leave a sketch pad to draw images from the dream. Whichever method you use, place your pad of paper, tape recorder or phone nearby so that you can easily get at it - preferably without having to get out of bed. If you use a journal, please leave room on the paper to add notes and/or pictures.

3. Be ready

90 percent of a dream can be lost in as little as 10 minutes of waking. If you awaken during the night with a dream memory, jot it down no matter how fuzzy it may seem. Most times this will be sufficient to stimulate fuller recollection of the dream upon waking.

4. Holding onto your dream

When you awake in the morning, try not to jump out of bed immediately. Stay in bed. Relax. Stay soft. Close your eyes and re-tell the dream to yourself. Start recording what you remember. Cling to any mood, feelings or image fragments and try to rebuild the story from them. Record all you can.

5. Don't judge

Let's face it, sometimes we don't like our dreams. We may even dismiss them or worse repress them. Remember they are *your* dreams; they have messages of healing specifically for you. Let them speak!

6. Share your dream

The benefits of sharing dreams may be difficult to describe to those who are not familiar with investigating their own dreams. A recent study on the cognitive, emotional, and creative benefits of dreaming found that not only did positive effects occur with recalling dreams but also after working with these dreams with group in a dream circle.[22]

My own experience overwhelmingly supports this.

Dreams have multiple layers of meaning. When we share our dreams with other people, family or friends, we can gain insights about ourselves. The telling of a dream to someone else helps us garner fresh perspective and discover additional meaning of our dreams. This can help solve problems, detoxify nightmares, and grow in our awareness of deeper selves. Like all intimate gatherings, we must feel it is a safe environment to share. Be sure that all members of the dream group respect each other's dreams and maintain the confidentiality of the dreams.

Finally, if you do not recall any of your dreams at first, don't worry, it will happen. Dream recall takes practice. **Be patient**. The journey is so worth it!

ACKNOWLEDGEMENTS

Thank you for reading this book. It means you are connected to your dreams, which is always a healthy thing.

First and foremost, I want to thank my dear, beautiful sister, Carole, who never doubted that this could happen. She read every line of each draft, making suggestions that improved those that followed. As a grammarian, there is none better. Her intuition about how to express ideas is always spot on as was her admonition to "read it aloud". This project helped me grow in many wonderful ways and having her be part of it was so amazing and rich. I cannot express enough words of gratitude to honor her.

Big hugs and thanks to my "phone dream group" and classmates who willingly tried out my guided exercise. The fruits of their participation were greater than I imagined. Thank you Debbie Baker, Mary Gossin Priore, and Candy Smith.

To Bob Haden, Founder of the Haden Institute, who visionary dream led to creation of a sanctuary for all those who wish to understand and honor their own dreams.

I am so grateful to the following people who either shared their dreams with me and/or offered up encouragement: Norm Betz, Taylor Button, Cathy Fields, Sharon Glass, Robert Hoss, Roberta Parker Martin, my dream mentor extraordinaire Diana McKendree, Jordan Ahava Olson, an exceptional dream artist, the talented musician and writer David Palmer, The Poetess Pam Pellegrino, Tammy Roth, John Rowe, and the Reverend Tom Wilson and his wife, Pat.

To my son, Quillan Snyder, the artist who designed the cover of this book, thank you for being so free with your dreams and your words of encouragement. You never cease to amaze me with your ability to cut through the noise and get to the heart of the matter. Thank you for giving me fresh eyes and challenging me.

Last but never least, to my soulmate and love of my life, Neil. Ever the cheerleader, you never doubt anything I decide to do. Love you gesweedie!

References & Endnotes

1   C. G. Jung, *Collected Works*, 18. Page 461.
2   C.G. Jung, *Letters* Vol II, pages 21-23.

Chapter 1

3   Schneider, Michael S. *A Beginners Guide to Constructing the Universe,* Mathematical Archetypes of Nature, Art and Science. New York: HarperCollins Publishers, 1994. XXVII.
4   Ibid.
5   http://www.Constitution.org/ime/hammurabi.htm
6   Bellos, Alex. *Alex Through the Looking Glass; How Life Reflects Numbers and Numbers Reflect Life.* London: Bloomsbury Publishing Plc, 2014. 6-7.
7   Ibid.
8   Kubovy, Micheal and Joseph Psotka, '*The Predominance of Seven and the Apparent Spontaneity of Numerical Choices*'; Journal of Experimental Psychology: Human Perception and Performance, Vol. 2, No 2, 1976. 291-294.

Chapter 2

9   Jung, Carl Gustav. *Collected Works* Vol 4 & 8 Translated by R.F.C. Hull. NYC: Pantheon Books, 1961. 456-458.

Because of his advancing age, Jung was unable to explore further into number archetypes, so he handed his notes to his close colleague, Marie-Louise von Franz who extended this work in her book, *Number and Time*. Evanston: Northwestern University Press, 1974. In Number and Time Von Franz clarifies and develops the archetypal hypothesis of Jung and Pauli. From her investigation, von Franz concluded that natural numbers represent the universal, recurring motion patterns of both psychic and physical energy. This means that motions patterns engender thought and structure models in the human psyche, which can be applied to physical phenomena and achieve relative congruence. It is probably what makes all conscious knowledge of nature possible.
10   Jung, Carol Gustav. *Collected Works* Vol 8, 1961. 870.
11   Ibid.
12   http://www.soulcraft.co/essays/the_12_common_archetypes.html. Carl Golden.

13 Jung, Carl Gustav. *'The Structure of the Unconscious', Collected Works* Vol 7. Princeton: Princeton University Press, 1953. 437-507.

14 Jung, Carl Gustav. *Man & His Symbols*. NY: Dell Publishing, 1964. 57.

15 Dreamhawk.com/dream-encyclopedia/archetype-of-the-great-mother.

16 Jung, Carl Gustav. *The Archetypes and The Collective Unconscious.* Princeton, NJ: Princeton University Press. 1959. Part II, page 73-110.

17 Ibid.

18 www.corecounseling.ca/archetypes-myth/the-archetypeal-father. Diane Hancox.

19 www -history.mcs.stand.ac.uk/Biographies/Pythagoras.html

20 Jung, C.G. *Memories, Dreams Reflections,* NY: Vintage Books, 1989. 195-196.

21 Bellos, Alex. *Alex Through the Looking Class;. How Life Reflects Numbers and Numbers Reflect Life.* NY: Bloomsbury,2014. 16-17.

22 http://dreamstudies.org/2014/01/24/new-empirical-support-for-the-value-of-dream-sharing/

Other Reference Material

Books On Jung & Archetypes:
Man & His Symbols edited by Carl G. Jung
The Portable Jung edited by Joseph Campbell
Dreams by C.G. Jung translated by R.F.C. Hull
The Archetypes and the Collective Unconscious by C.G. Jung translated by R.F.C. Hull
Jungian Archetypes by Robin Robertson

Websites on Jung & Archetypes:
http:www.integralscience.org/psyche-physis.html
www.goertzel.org/dynapsyc/1996/natphil.html

Books On the Meaning of Numbers:
Dream Language: Self-Understanding through Imagery and Color by Robert J. Hoss
Master Numbers: Cycles of Divine Order by Faith Javane
Sacred Number: The Secret Qualities of Quantities by Miranda Lundy
Deciphering the Cosmic Number by Arthur I. Miller
The Mystery of Numbers by Anne-Marie Schimmel
Born On A Blue Day by Daniel Tammet

Books On Numerology:
Numerology: The Complete Guide by Matthew Oliver Goodwin
The Complete Book of Numerology by David A. Phillips

WebSites on Numerology:
http://psychicjoanne.hubpages.com/hub/Numerology-meaning of numbers
http://www.2012-spiritual-growth-prophecies.com/numerology-meanings.html
http://theawanenedstate.tumblr.com/Numerology